D1717216

What's Inside?

Race Cars

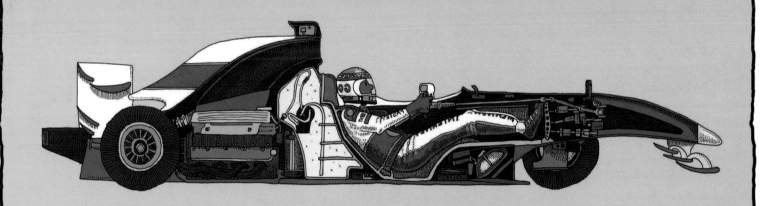

A⁺

Smart Apple Media

Published by Smart Apple Media, an imprint of Black Rabbit Books
P.O. Box 3263, Mankato, Minnesota 56002
www.blackrabbitbooks.com

Produced by David West   Children's Books
6 Princeton Court, 55 Felsham Road, London SW15 1AZ

Designed and illustrated by David West

Cataloging-in-Publication data is on file with the Library of Congress.
ISBN 978-1-62588-403-9
eBook ISBN 978-1-62588-432-9

Printed in China
CPSIA compliance information: DWCB16CP
010116

9 8 7 6 5 4 3 2 1

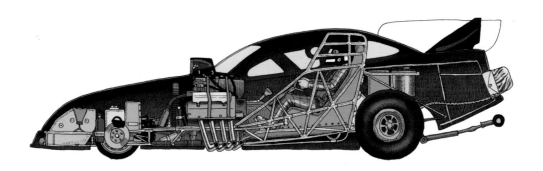

Contents

First Race Cars

Car racing began in the 1880s. These cars could not go very fast.

Wheels

1903 Mercedes

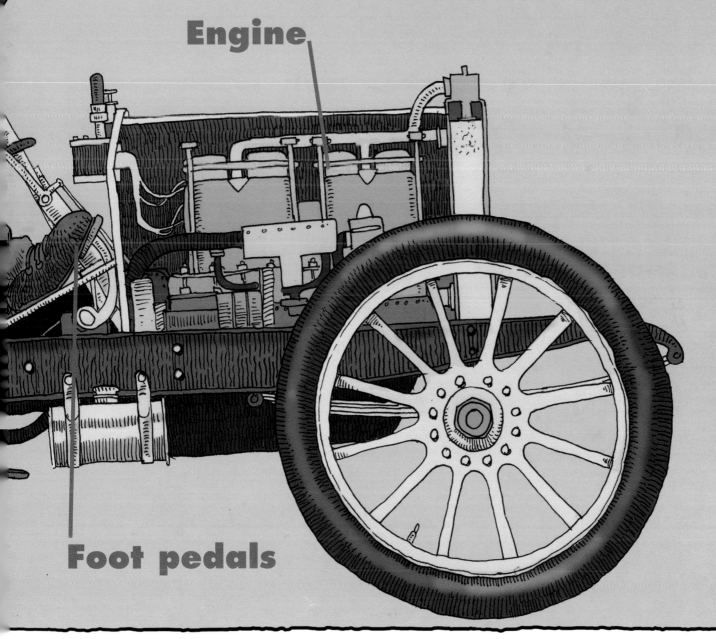

Engine

Foot pedals

One-Seat Racers

Race cars with one seat were made in the 1930s. The cars were light, so they could go faster.

Alfa Romeo P3

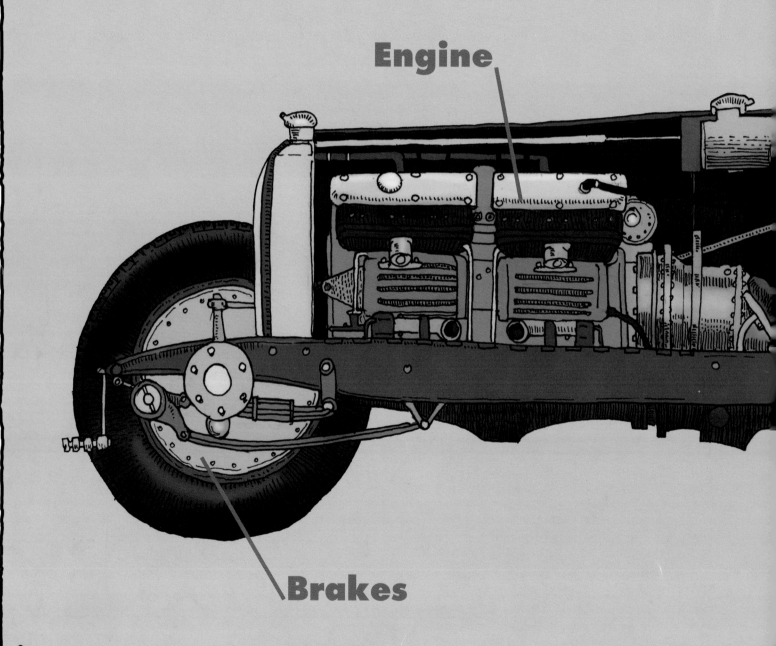

Engine

Brakes

Wheels

Race Cars Today

Race cars now have wheels outside the car bodies. They are built to go very fast.

Formula 1 Car

Steering wheel

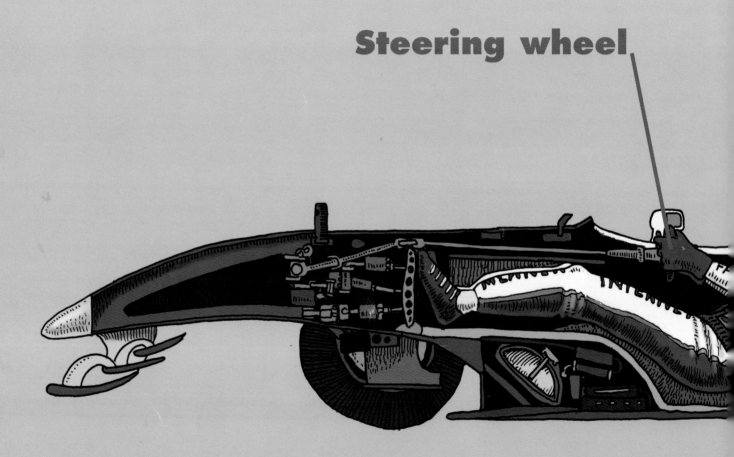

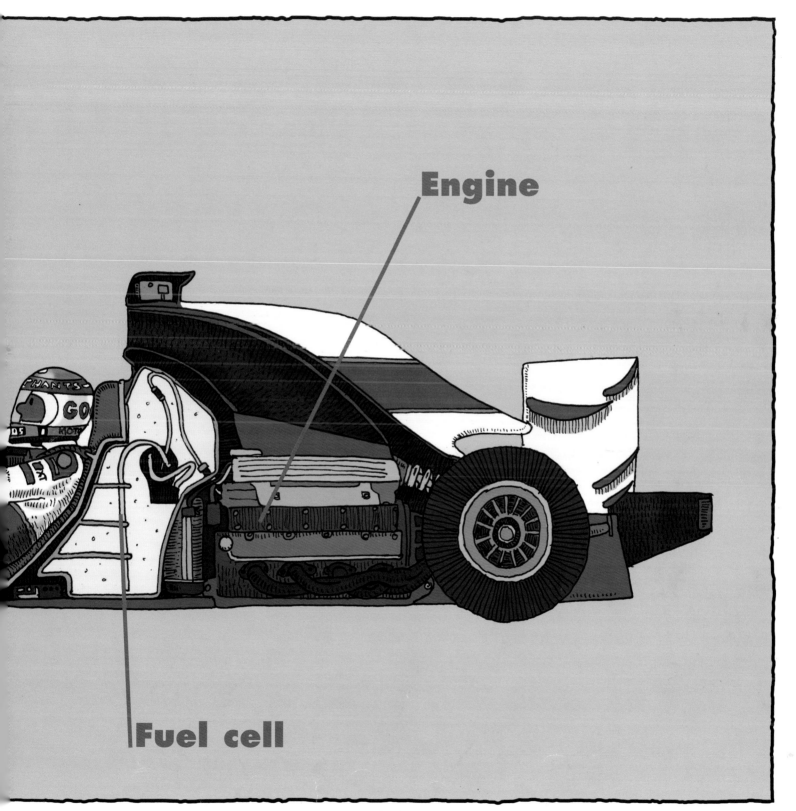

Engine

Fuel cell

Stock Cars

Stock cars are made just for racing. They all have the same type of engine.

NASCAR Stock Car

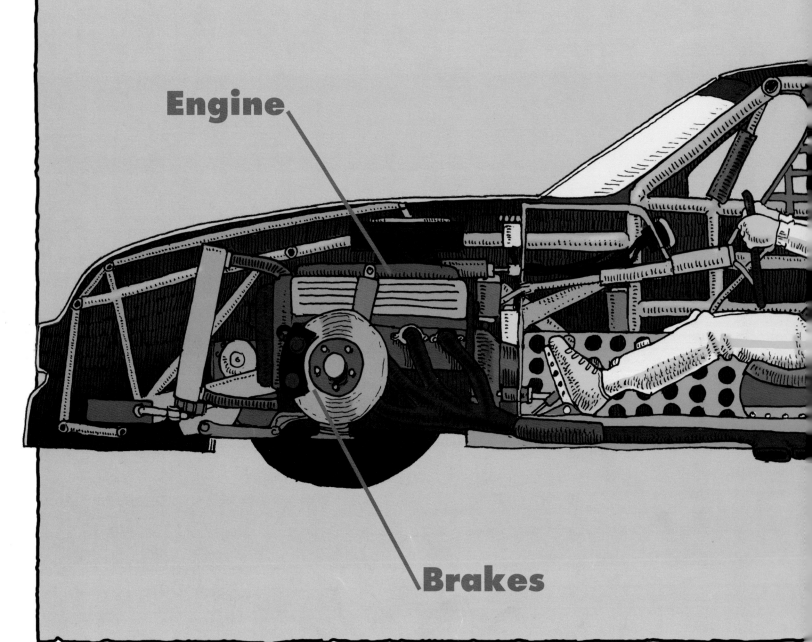

Engine

Brakes

Fuel tank

Drag Racers

Dragsters race down a short, straight track. They can really fly!

Funny Car

Engine

Fuel tank

Rear tire

Glossary

engine

A machine that makes something move

fuel

Material burned to create heat or power

race

A contest between people, animals, or vehicles to find out the fastest

track

A path or road used for racing

Index